To:_____

From:_____

Published by Sellers Publishing, Inc.
Copyright © 2013 Sellers Publshing, Inc
All rights reserved.

Sellers Publishing, Inc.
161 John Roberts Road, South Portland, Maine 04106
Visit our Web site: www.sellerspublishing.com
E-mail: rsp@rsvp.com

ISBN 13: 978-1-4162-0665-1

10 9 8 7 6 5 4 3 2 1

Printed and bound in China.

That's What She Said!

more than 150 witty sayings from funny women and movie legends

SELLERS
PUBLISHING

Chapter One

Who Needs Men?

"If it has tires or testicles, you're going to have trouble with it."

— Linda Furney

"Men aren't necessities. They're luxuries."

— Cher

"A man in the house is worth two in the street."

— Mae West

"Why did God create men? Because vibrators can't mow the lawn."

— Madonna

"Man invented language to satisfy his deep need to complain."

— Lily Tomlin

"A woman needs a man like a fish needs a net."

— Cynthia Heimel

"Summer bachelors, like summer breezes, are never as cool as they pretend to be."

— Nora Ephron

"Some of us are becoming the men we want to marry."

— Gloria Steinem

"Why is that men can be bastards and women must wear pearls and smile?"

— Lynn Hecht Schafran

"The more I know about men the more I like dogs."

— Gloria Allred

"I wish all men were like dogs."

— Halle Berry

"Some of my best leading men have been dogs and horses."

— Elizabeth Taylor

"Our perfect companions never have fewer than four feet."

— Colette

"Men should be like Kleenex: soft, strong and disposable."

— Cher

"We have reason to believe that man first walked upright to free his hands for masturbation."

— Lily Tomlin

"Men can read maps better than women. 'Cause only the male mind could conceive of one inch equaling one hundred miles."

— Roseanne Barr

"My attitude toward men who mess around is simple: If you find 'em, kill 'em."

— Loretta Lynn

"Men are like fine wine. They all start out like grapes, and it's our job to stomp them and keep them in the dark until they mature into something you'd like to have dinner with. "
— Kathleen Mifsud

"A woman without a man cannot meet a man, any man, of any age, without thinking, even if it's for a half second, 'Perhaps this is *the* man.'"
— Doris Lessing

"Can you imagine a world without men? No crime and lots of happy fat women."

— Nicole Hollander

"I've been on so many blind dates, I should get a free dog."

— Wendy Liebman

"I wanted to make it really special on Valentine's Day, so I tied my boyfriend up. And for three solid hours I watched whatever I wanted on TV."

— Tracy Smith

Chapter Two

Let's Get Physical

"Women might be able to fake orgasms.
But men can fake whole relationships."
— Sharon Stone

"It's not the men in my life that count, it's the life in my men."

— Mae West

"I carried my Oscar® to bed with me. My first and only three-way happened that night."

— Halle Berry

"Any woman who thinks the way to a man's heart is through his stomach is aiming about 10 inches too high."

— Adrienne Gusoff

"It's ill-becoming for an old broad to sing about how bad she wants it. But occasionally we do."

— Lena Horne

"I blame my mother for my poor sex life. All she told me was 'the man goes on top and the woman underneath.' For three years my husband and I slept in bunk beds."

— Joan Rivers

"The most important thing in acting is to be able to laugh and cry. If I have to cry, I think of my sex life. If I have to laugh, I think of my sex life."

— Glenda Jackson

"Sex appeal is 50% what you've got and 50% what people think you've got."

— Sophia Loren

Chapter Three

Love Actually

"If it is your time, love will track you down like a cruise missile."

— Lynda Barry

"If love is the answer, can you rephrase the question?"

— Lily Tomlin

"I don't want to live, I want to love first and live incidentally."

— Zelda Fitzgerald

"What's the difference between a boyfriend and a husband? About 30 pounds."

— Cindy Gardner

"I change my mind so much I need two boyfriends and a girlfriend."

— Pink

"Love is an electric blanket with somebody else in control of the switch."

— Cathy Carlyle

"Love is like the measles. The older you get it, the worse the attack."

— Mary Roberts Rinehart

That's What Miss Piggy Said...

" Is there a cure for a broken heart? Only time can heal your broken heart, just as time can heal his broken arms and legs. "

" When you are in love with someone you want to be near him all the time, except when you are out buying things and charging them to him. "

Chapter Four

Then Comes Marriage

"Marriage is a great institution, but I'm not ready for an institution yet."
— Mae West

" I am a very committed wife. And I should be committed too — for being married so many times. "

— Elizabeth Taylor

" Why can't women tell jokes? Because we marry them! "

— Kathy Lette

" I wish someone would have told me, that just because I'm a girl, I don't have to get married. "

— Marlo Thomas

" Marriage is like twirling a baton, turning hand-springs, or eating with chopsticks. It looks easy until you try it. "

— Helen Rowland

"Some women pick men to marry — and others pick them to pieces."

— Mae West

"The best way to get most husbands to do something is to suggest that perhaps they're too old to do it."

— Anne Bancroft

"When he's late for dinner, I know he's either having an affair or is lying dead in the street. I always hope it's the street."

— Jessica Tandy

"The trouble with some women is that they get all excited about nothing — and then marry him."
— Cher

"Marrying a man is like buying something you've been admiring for a long time in a shop window. You may love it when you get it home, but it doesn't always go with everything else in the house."
— Jean Kerr

"When a man brings his wife flowers for no reason, there's a reason."
— Molly McGee

"If love means never having to say you're sorry, then marriage means always having to say everything twice. Husbands, due to an unknown quirk of the universe, never hear you the first time."

— Estelle Getty

"I never married because I have three pets at home that answer the same purpose as a husband. I have a dog that growls every morning, a parrot that swears all afternoon, and a cat that comes home late at night."

— Marie Corelli

Chapter Five

Kidding Around

"Ask your child what he wants for dinner only if he's buying."

— Fran Lebowitz

"Adolescence is perhaps nature's way of preparing parents to welcome the empty nest."
— Karen Savage & Patricia Adams

"The invention of the teenager was a mistake. Once you identify a period of life in which people get to stay out late but don't have to pay taxes — naturally, no one wants to live any other way."
— Judith Martin

"If pregnancy were a book, they would cut the last two chapters."

— Nora Ephron

"Personally, I think any more than two or three kids is not a family, it's a litter."

— Tracey Ullman

"Tranquilizers work only if you follow the advice on the bottle — keep away from children."

— Phyllis Diller

"Giving birth is like taking your lower lip and forcing it over your head."

— Carol Burnett

"The best way to keep children home is to make the home atmosphere pleasant — and let the air out of the tires."

— Dorothy Parker

"Always be nice to your children, because they are the ones who will choose your rest home."

— Phyllis Diller

"Any mother could perform the jobs of several air traffic controllers with ease."

— Lisa Alther

Chapter Six

Working Girls

"Being a woman is hard work."

— Maya Angelou

"Girls just want to have funds."

— Adrienne Gusoff

"The phrase 'working mother' is redundant."

— Jane Sellman

"Always suspect any job men willingly vacate for women."

— Jill Tweedie

"Be different, stand out, and work your butt off."
— Reba McEntire

"When you see what some girls marry, you realize how they must hate to work for a living."
— Helen Rowland

"Somewhere out in this audience may even be someone who will one day follow in my footsteps, and preside over the White House as the president's spouse. I wish him well!"
— Barbara Bush

Chapter Seven

Domestic Diva?

"I'm not going to vacuum until Sears makes one you can ride on."
— Roseanne Barr

"I hate housework! You make the beds, you do the dishes, and six months later you have to start all over again."

— Joan Rivers

"When it comes to housework, the one thing no book of household management can ever tell you is how to begin. Or maybe I mean why."

— Katharine Whitehorn

"Housework can't kill you, but why take a chance?"
— Phyllis Diller

"For a single woman, preparing for company
means wiping the lipstick off the milk carton."
— Elayne Boosler

"Nature abhors a vacuum. And so do I."
— Anne Gibbons

Chapter Eight

Shop Till You Drop

"I shop, therefore I am."
— Tammy Faye Bakker

"The quickest way to know a woman is to go shopping with her." — Marcelene Cox

"Shopping is better than sex. At least if you're not satisfied, you can exchange it for something you really like." — Adrienne Gusoff

"You can't put a price tag on love, but you can on all its accessories." — Melanie Clark

"Thank God we're living in a country where the sky's the limit, the stores are open late, and you can shop in bed thanks to television."

— Joan Rivers

"The first time you buy a house you think how pretty it is and sign the check. The second time you look to see if the basement has termites. It's the same with men."

— Lupe Vélez

Chapter Nine

Food, Glorious Food

"Food is an important part of a balanced diet."
— Fran Lebowitz

"Never eat more than you can lift."

— Miss Piggy

"I think every woman should have a blowtorch."

— Julia Child

"Everything you see I owe to spaghetti."

— Sophia Loren

"Best way to get rid of kitchen odors: Eat out."
— Phyllis Diller

"One cannot think well, love well, sleep well, if one has not dined well."
— Virginia Woolf

"A good cook is like a sorceress who dispenses happiness."
— Elsa Schiaparelli

"Why does Sea World have a seafood restaurant? I'm halfway through my fishburger and I realize, oh my God, I could be eating a slow learner."

— Lynda Montgomery

"My weaknesses have always been food and men — in that order."

— Dolly Parton

Chapter Ten

The Way You Look . . .

"Outside every thin girl is a fat man trying to get in."

— Katharine Whitehorn

"I really don't think I need buns of steel. I'd be happy with buns of cinnamon."

— Ellen DeGeneres

"If high heels were so wonderful, men would be wearing them."

— Sue Grafton

"Until you're ready to look foolish, you'll never have the possibility of being great."

— Cher

"A lot of guys think the larger a woman's breasts are, the less intelligent she is. I don't think it works like that. I think it's the opposite. I think the larger a woman's breasts are, the less intelligent men become."

— Anita Wise

"The only rule is don't be boring and dress cute wherever you go. Life is too short to blend in."

— Paris Hilton

"A woman's dress should be like a barbed-wire fence: serving its purpose without obstructing the view."

— Sophia Loren

"I base most of my fashion taste on what doesn't itch."

— Gilda Radner

"Dress shabbily and they remember the dress; dress impeccably and they remember the woman."

— Coco Chanel

"You start out happy that you have no hips or boobs. All of a sudden you get them, and it feels sloppy. Then just when you start liking them, they start drooping."

— Cindy Crawford

"The reason the all-American boy prefers beauty over brains is that the all-American boy can see better than he can think."

— Farrah Fawcett

"I'm not offended by all the dumb-blonde jokes because I know I'm not dumb . . . and I also know that I'm not blonde."

— Dolly Parton

"I don't understand sizes anymore. There's a size zero, which I didn't even know that they had. It must stand for: 'Ohhh my God, you're thin.'"

— Ellen DeGeneres

"I have flabby thighs, but fortunately my stomach covers them."

— Joan Rivers

"If truth is beauty, how come no one has their hair done in the library?"

— Lily Tomlin

"Putting outfits together soothes me. Accessorizing is balm to my soul. If I can't save the world, I sure can make it pretty."

— Karen Marie Moning

"What do I wear in bed? Why, Chanel No. 5, of course."

— Marilyn Monroe

Chapter Eleven

Life Is Hell

"Living hell is the best revenge."

— Adrienne Gusoff

"In hell all the messages you ever left on answering machines will be played back to you."

— Judy Horacek

"What fresh hell is this?"

— Dorothy Parker

"Ever notice that 'what the hell' is always the right decision?"

— Marilyn Monroe

"If the world were a logical place, men would ride sidesaddle."

— Rita Mae Brown

"Life is hard. After all, it kills you."

— Katharine Hepburn

"I love to see a young girl go out and grab the world by the lapels. Life's a bitch. You've got to go out and kick ass."

— Maya Angelou

"Whatever you do, don't give up. Because all you can do once you've given up is bitch. I've known some great bitchers in my time. With some it's a passion, with others an art."

— Molly Ivins

"Save some for therapy."

— Rosie O'Donnell

Chapter Twelve

Talkin' 'Bout Bad Girls

"Lead me not into temptation; I can find the way myself."

— Rita Mae Brown

"It's the good girls who keep diaries; the bad girls never have the time."

— Tallulah Bankhead

"I used to be Snow White, but I drifted."

— Mae West

"You will do foolish things, but do them with enthusiasm."

— Colette

"For fast-acting relief, try slowing down."
— Lily Tomlin

"If I'd observed all the rules, I'd never have got anywhere."
— Marilyn Monroe

"Some say the glass is half empty, some say the glass is half full, I say, are you going to drink that?"
— Lisa Claymen

"A man can sleep around no questions asked, but if a woman makes 19 or 20 mistakes, she's a tramp."

— Joan Rivers

"Every woman should have four pets in her life. A mink in her closet, a jaguar in her garage, a tiger in her bed, and a jackass who pays for everything."

— Paris Hilton

"I consider myself to be a pretty good judge of people . . . that's why I don't like any of them."
— Roseanne Barr

"Good girls go to heaven, bad girls go everywhere."
— Mae West

"I like to drive with my knees. Otherwise, how can I put on my lipstick and talk on the phone?"
— Sharon Stone

"How many husbands have I had? You mean apart from my own?"
— Zsa Zsa Gabor

That's What Madonna Said...

"I've had the same goal I've had ever since I was a girl. I want to rule the world."

"I'm tough, ambitious, and I know exactly what I want. If that makes me a bitch, okay."

"Sometimes you have to be a bitch to get things done."

"A lot of people are afraid to say what they want. That's why they don't get what they want."

Chapter Thirteen

Diamonds Are a Girl's Best Friend

" Big girls need big diamonds. "
— Elizabeth Taylor

"I never worry about diets. The only carrots that interest me are the number you get in a diamond."

— Mae West

"I never let a rhinestone go unturned."

— Dolly Parton

"Diamonds never leave you . . . men do!"

— Shirley Bassey

"I don't exercise. If God had wanted me to bend over, he would have put diamonds on the floor."

— Joan Rivers

Chapter Fourteen

Age Is a State of Mind

"Age is just a number. It's totally irrelevant unless, of course, you happen to be a bottle of wine."
— Joan Collins

"Men become much more attractive when they start looking older. But it doesn't do much for women, though we do have an advantage: makeup."

— Bette Davis

"An archaeologist is the best husband a woman can have. The older she gets, the more interested he is in her."

— Agatha Christie

"Looking 50 is great — if you're 60."

— Joan Rivers

"The secret of staying young is to live honestly, eat slowly, and lie about your age."

— Lucille Ball

"You have to stay in shape. My grandmother started walking five miles a day when she was 60. She's 97 today, and we don't know where the hell she is."

— Ellen DeGeneres

"I don't know how you feel about old age . . . but in my case I didn't even see it coming. It hit me from the rear."

— Phyllis Diller

“The lovely thing about being 40 is that you can appreciate 25-year-old men more. ”

— Colleen McCullough

“Another belief of mine: that everyone else my age is an adult, whereas I am merely in disguise. ”

— Margaret Atwood

“I'm aiming by the time I'm 50 to stop being an adolescent. ”

— Wendy Cope

Chapter Fifteen

Getting the Last Word

"For most of history, Anonymous was a woman."
— Virginia Woolf

"To succeed in life, you need three things: a wishbone, a backbone, and a funny bone."
— Reba McEntire

"Good judgment comes from experience, and experience comes from bad judgment."
— Rita Mae Brown

"Never complain. Never explain."
— Katharine Hepburn

"I have a mouth and I'm not afraid to use it."
— Megan Fox